Leaning In, Letting Go

A Lenten Devotional

NICOLE MASSIE MARTIN

chalice
press

Saint Louis, Missouri

An imprint of Christian Board of Publication

Copyright ©2018 by Nicole Massie Martin

Bible quotations, unless otherwise noted, are from the *New Revised Standard Version Bible,* copyright 1989, Division of Christian Education of the National Council of the Churches of Christ in the United States of America. Used by permission. All rights reserved.

Cover art: © dreamstime

Print: 9780827221895 • EPUB: 9780827221901
EPDF: 9780827221918

ChalicePress.com

Printed in the United States of America

Dear readers,

I want to invite you on a journey that just might change your life. This is a journey with Christ through the cross to resurrection. For some of you, this is a familiar pathway. For others, this will be a new start. But no matter how many times you've been here, there are a few things we must let go along the way.

Throughout life, we've collected quite a bit of stuff we don't need. We have picked up bitterness from disappointment and a bit of anxiety from our need to control. We have packed some anger from unmet expectations and brought along some fear from the past. Yet this Lenten journey will not be as effective if we cannot leave those behind.

Leaning in to God and letting go of these unnecessary burdens go hand in hand. This series of short devotionals written just for you will help with the process of leaning in and letting go. The scripture texts are drawn from the Revised Common Lectionary Daily Readings, Year C and are listed in the New Revised Standard Version. In order to make the most of the next seven weeks, it would be good to establish a rhythm of daily silence, reading, prayer, and meditation that suits your lifestyle.

Please be prepared; leaning in can be a scary thing. You may notice things about God, and about yourself, that you did not notice before. We may take a few paces on the journey and find that the first glimpse of stress tempts us to pick up all that we put down. But the calling of Christ during this Lenten season is to lean into the fullness of God and let go of anything that hinders your progress.

For the next 48 days, we are taking a journey that will lead us to experience Christ like never before. We will lean in to see his sufferings and experience God's grace. We will lean in to witness Jesus' passion and make room for divine healing. When we lean in, we let go. And who knows? We just might see a better version of ourselves emerge on the other side.

So, start unpacking and let's get ready to go. Your life-changing journey awaits.

Your fellow traveler in Christ,
Nicole Massie Martin

ASH WEDNESDAY

Starting with "Why?"

Read Matthew 6:1–6, 16–21

"Beware of practicing your piety before others in order to be seen by them; for then you have no reward from your Father in heaven." (6:1)

"I can't have dessert; I'm fasting." My friend was so pleased with her denial that I almost felt a tinge of guilt as I gobbled my chocolate cake. I was proud that she decided to make a commitment to God and happy for her discipline, especially around cake.

As we left our time together that day, I couldn't stop thinking about her comment and how it made me feel. I was both happy and ashamed, inspired and embarrassed, all at the same time. Should I have been fasting too?

Public displays of righteousness often seem to have this effect. They make the "righteous" feel good while simultaneously making the "unrighteous" feel bad. However, Jesus was not interested in public works. He told his disciples that those people get on earth exactly what they want: to be seen by people on earth. But he wanted them to strive for something more than temporary satisfaction. Jesus wanted them to have a relationship with God in which their *doing* came as a result of their *being*. He was less concerned about *what* they were doing and more concerned about *why*.

As we enter this season of Lent, Jesus reminds us that he is more concerned about *why* we lean in than he is about *what* we let go. We are invited to fast, serve, and pray not because we'll be recognized by people, but because of our love for God. When God is our audience, no one else has to know.

So whether we choose to eat cake or deny it, whether celebrating in silence or with a loud song, God is most concerned with our motivation, not our activation. When we have the right motives, the simple act of leaning in will be all the reward we need.

Lord, help us to let go of outward piety and lean into your unfailing love. Let your presence be our pursuit and your pleasure our only reward.

FIRST THURSDAY

Expect the Unexpected

Read Exodus 5:10–23

Then Moses turned again to the Lord and said, "O Lord, why have you mistreated this people? Why did you ever send me? Since I first came to Pharaoh to speak in your name, he has mistreated this people, and you have done nothing at all to deliver your people." (5:22–23)

It was supposed to be different. When Moses agreed to follow God, things were supposed to get better. The lives of the Israelites should have gotten better. Moses and his family should have been better off. Saying "yes" to God was supposed to lead to increase, not decrease. But instead of getting better, things began to get worse.

God met with Moses and promised to deliver the Israelites. God promised they would be free to worship and no longer bound to the Egyptians. But Pharaoh denied the request for worship and decided to make their lives worse. Demanding more bricks with less straw, the promise of freedom instantly turned into the reinforcement of slavery. Is this what God had in mind all along?

Life with God is filled with promises and expectations. However, God's promises are not always fulfilled when or how we expect. We can be so focused on an expected result of a promise that we lose sight of the source of the promise. In our anguish, we want God to move quickly, wasting no time to do what God promised to do. Yet even in desperate times, we are called to reset our expectations of God. This becomes a sacred opportunity to take the focus off of what God does and refocus on who God is.

What expectations must you surrender today? How can you redirect your attention from what God does to who God is? When you lean in, you might be surprised how God allows you to let go. While your assignment or suffering may not immediately change, God can strengthen you to let go of the resentment associated with your pain. Leaning in helps us to discover that our trouble does not trouble God one bit.

God, reset my expectations. Shift my gaze from your hands to your heart and carry me through all my troubles. Thank you for teaching me how to wait on you.

FIRST FRIDAY

Accepting the Flight

Read Psalm 91

Because you have made the Lord *your refuge, the Most High your dwelling place, no evil shall befall you, no scourge come near your tent. (91:9–10)*

We are living in the midst of a refugee crisis. Around the world, thousands of men, women, and children are fleeing their homes to save their lives. Their flight is not about luxury, but safety. Driven to desperation, these families will do anything and go almost anywhere to keep themselves alive.

The pursuit of life in a new land is not a naïve one. Those who are forced to leave understand that there are no guarantees on the other side. Yet the intensity of suffering that would come with staying leaves them little choice. They either stay with the guarantee of trouble, or go with the possibility of peace.

Although we may not be personally familiar with this experience, our faith compels us to understand this complex reality. To say that God is our refuge implies that we are refugees in some way. Without minimizing the trauma of this flight, it can be said that we all have things, places, and even people from which we have to flee in order to save our lives. In these times, the truth of God-as-refuge comes alive.

God is our dwelling, and in God's presence we experience protection from danger. This does not mean that we are exempt from trouble. On the contrary, many would argue that being a believer invites tremendous amounts of suffering and trouble. Yet when faced with the guarantee of trouble outside of God's presence, or the assurance of peace within God's presence, we would rather find refuge in the Lord, even if it costs us our lives.

From what or whom must you flee in order to experience the safety of God's presence today? God yearns to be our refuge, and all are welcomed in.

Lord, we pray for your covering and protection for refugees around the world. May our solidarity with them remind us of our status in this world until you come for us again.

FIRST SATURDAY

Seek and Find

Read John 12:28–36

"While you have the light, believe in the light, so that you may become children of light." After Jesus had said this, he departed and hid from them. (12:36)

My girls love playing hide-and-seek. But at ages three and five, they're not very good at it. They try to hide behind a door, but their clothes tend to peek out. They may crouch behind the sofa when we're coming into the living room, but their giggles always give them away. With them, it's not so much "hide and seek" as it is "seek and find." They enjoy the game simply because they love being found.

It could be argued that Jesus enjoyed playing "seek and find" as well. Even when his hiding places were good, Jesus proved consistently that he loved being found by those who sought him. In this text, Jesus gladly revealed himself as the Son of Man, despite the fact that people didn't fully understand what that meant. It's as if Jesus was hiding right in front of them. But he didn't remain hidden. He wanted to be found *in them*. Jesus was inviting his disciples to a game of "seek and find" that would end with the light being found in them.

While we may outgrow the game, we never outgrow the practice of searching for God. At times, our search may be obstructed by darkness. Suffering and sorrow, pain and disbelief can all tamp down the light, threatening to snuff it out completely. Thank God for the Son of man, whose light outshines the darkness.

Today, we lean into this divine light with great anticipation. We let go of our need to hide, and lean into the joy of being found by Christ. By rekindling our awe of God's Holy Light and reclaiming our belief in Jesus as the Light, we will burn again with passion for the One who seeks and finds us all.

Lord, we earnestly seek you in the darkness. Help us to find you as the light so that we may find life as children of that light. We cannot shine without you.

FIRST SUNDAY

Closer Than Close

Read Romans 10:5–13

..."*The word is near you, on your lips and in your heart*"... *(10:8)*

Before there was travel-sized, there was Jesus. Able to fit in your mouth and your heart, Jesus proves his ability to go with us everywhere at all times, in the form of God's Word, through the power of the Holy Spirit. John says that Jesus was the Word who was in the beginning with God and was God, becoming flesh and dwelling among us (John 1:1,14). In this miraculous way, Jesus, through the Spirit, makes God and God's Word portable, residing in and around us through confession and belief.

But why don't we feel this closeness all the time? What is it about God's Word that makes Jesus feel so distant at times, so far removed from where we are? Perhaps we fall into the traps suggested by the apostle Paul in the preceding verses from chapter 10 of his letter to the early Christians in Rome. Just before verse eight, Paul cautions believers against trying to ascend to the heavens to bring Christ down, or descend to the depths to bring Christ up (6–7).

When faced with the contemporary issues of the world, we may wrongly assume that God's Word is irrelevant. When we need guidance or direction, we might be tempted to think God's Word is too complicated to understand. Instead, Paul suggests that the Lord is neither out of reach nor out of touch. The Word is neither too sacred nor too material, but alive and closer than we think. In an effort to draw us into an intimate relationship, God came close and dares to live in the messiness of our lives.

The portability of the Gospel reminds us of the intentions of God's heart. Jesus demonstrates that God never intended to be far away; God always intended to be close. When we remove the barriers that keep us from the Word, we are free to worship and love God through regular engagement with scripture. Perhaps then we'll recognize that what we need most is not beyond us, but right here within.

Lord, we need to feel you close. Teach us to engage with your Word so that we can feel the beat of your heart.

FIRST MONDAY

Choose Mercy

Read 1 Chronicles 21:1–17

Then David said to Gad, "I am in great distress; let me fall into the hand of the Lord, *for his mercy is very great; but let me not fall into human hands." (21:13)*

"You can take back the rock, but it takes time to fix the window." These were the words of comfort my dad offered me after a terrible fight with my younger sister. I wasn't good at fighting with my hands, so I had learned how to fight with my words. I knew her soft spots and used my words to pierce in a way that could hurt more than a punch. I apologized, but she was still hurt. I was forgiven of the sin but still had to deal with the consequence.

We are forgiven of our sins by confession through Jesus Christ. In an instant, God's grace allows us to take back the rock. But sooner or later, we still have to deal with the broken window. David was no exception. Even as a man after God's own heart, King David sinned with an unsanctioned census. When he recognized what he had done, he prayed for forgiveness and took back the rock. But just like us, David still had to deal with the consequences.

Given the choice between God and man, the king chose the punishment that came from God's hand. While he could not avoid the consequence of his sin, he chose to lean on the mercy of God, even with the guarantee of suffering. In many ways, the choice to suffer in the hands of God was a foreshadowing of the price Jesus paid for all of us on the cross. Taking on the punishment for our sins, Jesus took back our rocks and mended the window of our relationship with God.

What rocks have you thrown and what windows have been broken? You are invited to bring your mistakes to God, knowing that there is nothing too big or too small for God to restore.

Gracious God, have mercy upon us. Forgive us of our sins and cleanse our unrighteousness. Thank you for restoring our lives and for making us whole in you.

FIRST TUESDAY

From Innocent Lips

Read Psalm 17

Hear a just cause, O Lord; attend to my cry; give ear to my prayer from lips free of deceit. From you let my vindication come; let your eyes see the right. (17:1–2)

God does not deny the call of the righteous. By virtue of God's goodness and as indicated by God's compassion, our Maker does not turn from the cries of the innocent. As echoed by the psalmist, we believe that God listens to the cries of the guiltless and vindicates the lives of those falsely accused. Yet this truth brings both comfort and conviction: comfort in knowing that God will bring justice for those in need, conviction in the fact that none of us are completely free from deceit.

Our humanity makes us vulnerable to sin. We were born in it and cannot find our way out alone. Sin traps us in a mirror maze where every turn takes us to another angle of ourselves, teasing us with a way out only to confront us with another view of our pain. In struggle, we cry out to God. In pain and torment, we pray for relief, knowing deep down that we are not worthy to receive the mercy and grace of a Holy God.

Who shall save us from our sin? Who will hear us when we cry out from lips tainted with deceit and hearts cloaked with shame? Jesus, our righteous Savior, will hear! He is the only truly innocent One, able to deliver us from ourselves and defend us against the attacks of our enemies.

Our confidence in the midst of crises comes from having Jesus as our covering. Our strength in struggle stems from having a relationship with the Righteous One. Although few, if any, can pray the prayer of this psalm, Jesus opens the door for all to pray through him for vindication and relief. Wrapped in the sacrifice of the Son, we have the assurance that God hears our prayer and is able to respond.

God, we confess that we do not always pray with clean lips. Purify our hearts and grant us the assurance of your protection and grace.

SECOND WEDNESDAY

Your Life Is Priceless

Read Luke 21:34–22:6

They were greatly pleased and agreed to give him money. So he consented and began to look for an opportunity to betray him to them when no crowd was present. (22:5–6)

"There are some things money can't buy. For everything else, there's Mastercard." This unforgettable slogan of the popular credit card company took off in the early 2000s. The advertising made us smile and feel good about things that money cannot buy. Simultaneously, they were buying the trust of consumers who would look to Mastercard as a brand with compassion, a card that understood the real values of the world.

The problem is that credit card companies can neither create nor define human values. It could be argued that the appeal of putting items that we cannot afford on a card that charges interest is, in itself, against human values. But this is the age-old attack of the enemy against God: to thwart the true values of God.

The same was true in the story of Judas. From the moment Satan entered him, he immediately set out to find ways to betray Jesus. The time he spent with God was priceless. Yet in the value system of the prince of this world, that all amounted to nothing more than 30 pieces of silver.

If we are not mindful, we, too, can devalue what God declares is priceless. We devalue our time with God and our relationship with the Lord in countless ways. Even worse, we devalue ourselves every time we deny our worth as image-bearers of our Holy King.

What would it look like for you to value what God values? Perhaps we can start with ourselves. In this season, Christ beckons us to come closer so that he may affirm our value through the price that was paid for us to become children of God. Jesus reminds us that our lives are priceless, not because of what we've done, but because of whose we are.

Jesus, there is no currency of this world that can pay for my life in and with you. Give me grace to remember my value and love to extend that value to all your people.

SECOND THURSDAY

Recalculating Loss and Gain

Read Philippians 3:2–12

Yet whatever gains I had, these I have come to regard as loss because of Christ. (3:7)

A higher gain can soothe almost any loss. I've had to learn this as a parent when I've had to say "no." For instance, turning off the television is always easier when I have something more fun for my children to do. The loss of what they want is often lessened when I can offer them something better.

The same can be said of us. Like children, we can journey through life on a treasure hunt, accumulating accomplishments like gems hidden on the path of success. We strive for position, titles, and power, and when we receive them, we long for more. Our egos drive us toward entitlement, keeping us from being content with anything less than what we think we should have. In addition, our culture nurtures these pursuits, affirming those who arrive and shaming those who do not.

But those who achieve what others so desperately desire prove what we refuse to see at first sight: that the treasures of this world can be empty and void. Cotton candy versions of fame that are sweet at first can quickly dissolve into nothing more than spoons full of sugar. We may yearn for what we see, but what is unseen in God can amount to so much more.

As we draw closer to God, we develop an appetite for what God desires. The more we taste of divine goodness, the more we crave it. When our needs meet up with God's provision, we recognize that what is natural through Christ is more valuable than what is manufactured by the world.

This journey toward the cross requires that we lean into heavenly riches and let go of earthly gains. When we do, we will begin to know Christ and experience the power of his resurrection.

Lord, give us strength to count everything as loss for the sake of knowing you. Help us to experience your resurrection and life.

SECOND FRIDAY

Find Faith in the Midst of Fear

Read Psalm 27

*The L*ord *is my light and my salvation; whom shall I fear? The L*ord *is the stronghold of my life; of whom shall I be afraid? (27:1)*

It's been said that "fear not" is the most repeated command in the Bible. It's also said that fear and anxiety are among the top causes of stress for Americans today. The combination of both creates a wonderful ebb and flow of complexity and grace.

On the one hand, we have so many reasons to fear. Having lived through recession, we fear the loss of jobs and financial instability. With repeated mass shootings and terrorist attacks, we fear tragedies that can strike at any time. The uncertainty of relationships creates fear in our marriages, and the fragility of life makes us fear sickness that leads to death.

On the other hand, David declared prophetically that we have nothing to fear. Were things easier for him? Sure, he may not have had the exact pressures we have, but his story indicates that he, too, had good reason to fear. His enemies were real. His family experienced conflict and broken relationships. He witnessed and experienced the effects of sickness and pain.

But David allowed the reality of God to supersede his fear. His problems and enemies were real, but he understood God to be bigger. David demonstrated how we can rise above our fears by leaning into God as our light, salvation, and strength. By seeking the Lord and dwelling in the temple, his faith grew in spite of his fears.

What would it look like for your faith to grow in spite of your fears? With the confidence of David and the gift of God's promises, we can rest in knowing that the love of God for us is greater than anything against us.

Lord, we acknowledge that we are genuinely afraid, but that you are genuinely with us. Let our knowledge of you surpass all else that we know. Help us to us cast off our fear and lean into confident faith.

SECOND SATURDAY

Exchanging Our Pride for His Passion

Read Matthew 23:37–39

"Jerusalem, Jerusalem, the city that kills the prophets and stones those sent to it! How often have I desired to gather your children together as a hen gathers her brood under her wings, and you were not willing!" (23:37)

Who would willingly reject the love of the Savior? None of us, if we knew who he was. Unfortunately, we don't always know those sent to save us, nor do we always understand the purpose behind every divine intervention. We can be prideful with our own ways, believing the vain words expressed in the famous poem *Invictus*, that we are the "masters of our fate" and the "captains of our souls."

Jesus was sent first to the children of Israel, but they did not receive him. To make matters worse, the teachers of the law and Pharisees who spent the most time in God's Word seemed to be the least concerned with actually following it. They were accused of hypocrisy: teaching the people one thing while practicing the opposite themselves. They wore the mask of pride in teaching and did not receive the Messiah when he appeared.

Yet rather than leave them condemned, Jesus lamented the condition of their souls. He grieved the loss of his people, reflecting on how often he longed to draw in the very ones intent on pushing him out. This passionate, unrequited love is paramount to the cross. Through Jesus, we see the steadfast compassion of God who desires to bring us close when our wills seek to drive God away.

Letting go of pride often involves recognizing the many times we, too, have rejected the Savior. We have all turned away from the redeeming hand of Christ, assuming we could handle our lives on our own. But despite our pride and hypocrisy, Jesus still longs to draw us in.

The Lenten season allows us to stand before Christ as vulnerable children. We don't have to be perfect, but we must be willing. We are part of God's brood, and our place is reserved under God's wings.

Lord, forgive us for allowing pride and hypocrisy to lead us astray. Remind us of your never-ending love and, by your grace, draw us close again.

SECOND SUNDAY

The Big Reveal

Read Luke 9:28–43a

When the voice had spoken, Jesus was found alone. And they kept silent and in those days told no one any of the things they had seen. (9:36)

Everyone loves superheroes. And while all superheroes are fascinating, not all of them are the same. Some are super because of wealth and technology, like Iron Man and Batman. Others are super because they were born on a different planet like Superman or in a mythical place on Earth like Wonder Woman and Black Panther. But the ones that capture my attention are those who are able to transform.

The ability to shift from regular to super, from ordinary to extraordinary, is a captivating gift. Their stories usually include some "big reveal" when they unveil the truth of their powers to those who never suspected who they were (think Lois Lane and Clark Kent, or Peter Parker and Mary Jane, to name a few). Once the secret is out, those who know are never the same. They are forever marked with the awe of knowing and the responsibility of protecting the secret.

Perhaps this is what happened to Peter, James, and John as they witnessed the transfiguration of Jesus. As he prayed, Jesus's face was transformed before them and his clothes became a dazzling white. Moses and Elijah appeared, a cloud of glory descended, the voice of God affirmed Christ the Son — and the disciples were absolutely terrified. But, after this "big reveal," all they saw was Jesus, the same one they had known all along.

How would our lives be different if we caught a glimpse of the glory of Christ? Would we recognize him as Lord, elevating him higher than our greatest heroes, or would we treat the revelation like comic entertainment that hardly affects how we live?

We will never experience the full glory of God's "big reveal" here on earth, but Jesus still longs to reveal glimpses of his truth to the world. The Savior was transfigured so that we might be transformed. As we lean into the cross, may we lean into Christ's glory in a way that changes us for good.

We praise you, Lord, for your infinite power. Teach us your truth and reveal your glory so that the world may know that Jesus reigns.

SECOND MONDAY

A Time to Mourn

Read Exodus 33:1–6

When the people heard these harsh words, they mourned, and no one put on ornaments. (33:4)

They were lost, so they made an idol. The golden calf represented so much of their pain. They felt abandoned by Moses and by God. They were impatient and frustrated by the delay in direction. They were prideful and believed they could contrive answers when none were given. The people of Israel were made to worship, and when Moses did not come down from the mountain when they thought he should, they made a calf and called it their god.

The LORD, so angry with this blasphemous act, threatened to completely destroy them. Only Moses could distill God's anger, and even then, they were afflicted by plague and forfeited God's presence as a companion to the Promised Land.

Before, they worshipped. Now, they mourned. But mourning was the most faithful and appropriate response the people could give to God. Celebration would have been empty, and thanksgiving would have seemed insincere. When they recognized the significance of their sin, the people mourned the loss of relationship and trust with the One who had brought them out of Egypt.

What does it look like to mourn for our sins today? As people of the new covenant, we bask in God's grace, knowing that Jesus has forgiven and redeemed us. But perhaps there are still times when mourning is the most faithful and appropriate response to a Holy God. When we express sorrow over our sin and grieve the sins of others, we step into a new layer of solidarity with the cross.

The Lenten season is about clinging to the cross in a way that causes our souls to grieve. In fasting, we surrender our right to rejoice and embrace opportunities to mourn. We do not become martyrs to replace the cross, but we walk in humility to understand the cross. In this sorrow, we more clearly see the redemption of the Savior.

Master, teach us how to mourn as a faithful response to sin and idolatry. Give us grace to grieve and strength to express sorrow. May we find our help in you.

SECOND TUESDAY

Praise Power

Read Psalm 105:1–42

O give thanks to the Lord, call on his name, make known his deeds among the peoples. (105:1)

Gratitude is a powerful antidote to despair. In the plethora of research around the art of being happy, scientists have discovered that giving thanks and expressing appreciation can literally change your mind. With praise and thanksgiving, you can move from angst to peace, from frustration to trust, and from gloom to glee in a matter of thoughts.

This has always been the biblical reality. The call to give thanks is often the call to remember. When we thank God, we remember who God is and reflect on all that God has done. In this psalm, the invitation to thanksgiving is an invitation to reminisce on God's goodness among the people throughout the generations. Above all, we are encouraged to celebrate the Lord who keeps the covenant.

Yet life has a way of provoking spiritual amnesia. When troubles arise, it's easy for us to forget God's faithfulness and overlook all that God alone has done. While we know in our minds that God is true to God's promises, we often struggle to believe this truth in our hearts.

As we walk the path toward a fuller life in Christ, ancient Israel encourages us to remember. Remember the God who never leaves nor forsakes. Remember God's faithfulness in deliverance and protection. Remember the ancient God who was and is, and is to come. When we truly remember, our gratitude becomes a natural reaction.

What stands in the way of your worship? How can you clear the path to walk with joy, even in suffering? In this season, we can lean more fully into praise and let go of whatever causes us to be ungrateful. We cannot get to know God without being drawn into praise of God. When life scatters stumbling blocks on the road, our praise, worship, and thanksgiving can clear the way.

We give you thanks, O Lord, for presence and power. Let our increased knowledge of you lead to an overflow of praise. No one is worthier than you.

THIRD WEDNESDAY

Feast Your Eyes

Read 2 Chronicles 20:1–22

"...We do not know what to do, but our eyes are on you." (20:12b)

The phrase "I don't know" is considered taboo in some spaces. After all, we don't build confidence in doctors or lawyers or teachers who do not know. For them, not knowing can be an admission of ignorance or an affirmation of incompetence. When people are paid to be experts, they literally cannot afford not to know.

In our information-driven society, it is difficult to be comfortable with the unknown. We thrive based on what we know and push toward the idea that almost everything can be known. But instead of finding strength in knowledge, we find anxiety in ambiguity.

This is especially true when it comes to our lives. We exhaust every ounce of our energy finding answers to what we'll do next, where we're headed now, or how we plan to get there as soon as possible. Without divine guidance, we can create empty solutions or, worse, end up taking the wrong path.

But Jehoshaphat teaches us that we don't need to know all the answers; we just need to know where to look. Threatened by the enemy and uncertain of the next steps, Jehoshaphat modeled what believers can do when we don't know what to do: look confidently to the Lord. By understanding what he did not know, he was able to lean on what he did know. Jehoshaphat may not have known the enemy, but he did know the promises of God's covenant protection.

What do you know about God that will ease the burden of what is unknown for your life? Take the pressure off of knowing and look confidently to Christ as the All-Knowing One. We look confidently, knowing that God will answer. We look patiently, willing to wait until God responds. Above all, we look expectantly, anticipating that what God directs for us will be better than any answer we can give on our own.

Lord, there are so many answers we do not know. Teach us to willingly engage your wisdom and to patiently wait for your response.

THIRD THURSDAY

The Fearless and The Faithful

Read Revelation 2:8–11

"Do not fear what you are about to suffer…Be faithful until death, and I will give you the crown of life." (2:10)

The passion behind his words was unforgettable. As I stood among hundreds of leaders from all over the world, I was moved to tears as the young man from Niger spoke about his future. The pastor who had brought him to Christ was murdered by a terrorist group, and there were threats against his life as well. He had been disowned by his family and forced into slavery for turning from his jihadist roots. But with all that was against him, this brave believer declared his allegiance to God. He was not afraid to suffer for the Gospel, and nothing could dissuade him from God's truth.

I listened to him and cried for so many reasons. I wept with pride for him, thanking God for the power of his witness. I cried for the eminent danger awaiting him and Christians like him around the world. But my tears were also for myself, not knowing how I would hold up under similar circumstances.

At this very moment, Christians around the world are suffering for the sake of Christ. Some are hung on literal crosses, like my neighbor from Vietnam. Some are sold into slavery, like children in India. Some are tortured in prisons, like the woman I met from Iran. The suffering may be different, but the source is the same: they suffer for their love of Christ.

The gift of this season is our willingness to be in solidarity with all who suffer for Christ around the world. As we seek to understand the pain and passion of Jesus, we can grow in our understanding of brothers and sisters who suffer as well. Their tears can become our tears, their pain our pain, and their sorrow our sorrow. In so doing, we prepare for the day when their joy will be our joy as Jesus comes for us again. We who remain faithful will share in collective celebration, delighting in the crown of eternal life with Christ.

God, we pray for those who are persecuted and for ourselves. Strengthen and sustain us, guide and keep us in the midst of suffering. Help us to remain faithful in anticipation of your heavenly reward.

THIRD FRIDAY

Quenching Soul-Thirst

Read Psalm 63

O God, you are my God, I seek you, my soul thirsts for you; my flesh faints for you, as in a dry and weary land where there is no water. (63:1)

By the time we feel thirsty, we are already in the early stages of becoming dehydrated. Thirst is the body's response to dehydration, triggering us to do something before it's too late. The mouth becomes dry, the tongue becomes heavy, and saliva thickens, making it hard to swallow and even hard to breathe. Thirst affects our stomachs and bowels, our skin and eyes, our heads and hearts. Without water, we cannot think, or speak, or move well, and if we get too dehydrated for too long, we can die.

The world can feel like a desert for the thirsty soul. When the soul thirsts, our work feels dry, our hearts become heavy, and our pain thickens, making it hard to focus on anything, including God. When we thirst, we can find ourselves running toward fanciful mirages, only to end up lapping the grainy emptiness of sand. We can easily be deceived, believing that anything wet will do. We can be sold sugary drinks that only leave us more dehydrated than when we began.

Soul-thirst can only be quenched by the Spirit. As David expressed in this psalm, the true yearnings of our souls can only be satisfied by the presence of God. When he encountered God's presence in the sanctuary and beheld God's power and glory, his soul began to sing. God was like water to David. He could not live without the Lord and could not stand the symptoms of being outside of God's presence.

Lent reminds us of the depth of our thirst. Like David, we still live in a dry and weary land where there is no water. Our jobs alone cannot quench us. Our relationships alone cannot satisfy us. In this season, we recognize now more than ever that the only One who can truly appease our thirst is Christ Jesus, our Lord.

Lord, quench our thirsty souls. Lead us to the deep well of your presence and purify our hearts with your love. Thank you for supplying our needs.

THIRD SATURDAY

Who's Bad?

Read Luke 6:43–45

"No good tree bears bad fruit, nor again does a bad tree bear good fruit; for each tree is known by its own fruit." (6:43–44a)

We like to think that the apple doesn't fall far from the tree. But sometimes it does. Not every child reflects his or her parent and not every parent is worth reflecting. Good people can do bad things and bad people can have capacity for good. A good seed planted doesn't guarantee good fruit, and every once in a while, a bad seed can bring a good harvest.

Depending on your vantage point, we are all walking contradictions: we're either good trees who sometimes bear bad fruit or we're bad trees who occasionally bear good fruit. Our good days pale in comparison to God's goodness, and our bad days reveal the depth of our depravity. Even the most holy among us do not always speak in hymns and songs, and our mouths betray the sin that dwells within our hearts.

Who will deliver us from this paradox of humanity? Thanks be to God for sending Jesus as the perfect Son of God and man. Jesus, our Savior, is the only good tree who bears good fruit. Christ is the only One whose heart is pure and whose mouth speaks words uncontaminated by sin. When we are in him and he is in us, we will find a solution for our human contradiction. Apart from him, we cannot bear fruit at all (John 15:5).

Today, we can let go of the pressure to manufacture what is good and allow Christ to bear his goodness in us. Our surrender to Christ reminds us that we are poor reflections of God without him. But there is joy for those who allow Jesus to be in us what we could never be by ourselves: an earnest reflection of God.

Lord, we can never be good apart from your goodness. We can never bear fruit without the seed of your Word. Tend the soil of our hearts and, by your mercy, make us more like you.

THIRD SUNDAY

Generous Grace

Read Isaiah 55:1–9

Ho, everyone who thirsts, come to the waters; and you that have no money, come, buy and eat! Come, buy wine and milk without money and without price. (55:1)

She was five cents short, but he paid for her entire meal. She was at the airport going home and a good Samaritan came out of nowhere, handed his card to the cashier, and said that everything was on him. On top of that, he gave her a few dollars to get an extra snack for her trip.

She stretched out her hand to give everything back to him. "This is too much," she said, not certain of what he would want in return for this unmerited kindness. "Please, take it," he answered with a smile. "God's been good to me this week." As she held the money in her hand and waited for her food, she was overcome with the weight of her unworthiness.

Unearned generosity can make us feel deeply unworthy. We've bought into a culture of reciprocity that can make us feel awful when we cannot participate in equal exchange. We know that it is better to give than to receive, but life is easier when our giving stays in stride with our receiving.

When we commence the journey of life with God, we enter a life of unparalleled generosity. Nothing that we give to God even comes close to what God gives to us. In the economy of God the covenant is our currency, and those in relationship with God are the wealthiest of all. We enjoy this luxury because of Jesus, who confirmed the covenant by giving his life in exchange for ours.

What do you need to release in order to lean into the generosity of God's love? Right now, God offers access to those who can't afford entry and allows us to purchase what we need without spending a dime. So do not waste another moment. Come now and enjoy the bountiful love of our gracious God.

Jesus, words cannot express how grateful we are for your sacrifice. Because of you, we can live in the abundance of life with God. Help us to model that generosity toward others as you have so graciously done for us.

THIRD MONDAY

The Weapon of Judgment

Read Romans 2:1–11

Therefore you have no excuse, whoever you are, when you judge others; for in passing judgment on another you condemn yourself, because you, the judge, are doing the very same things. (2:1)

The world makes it so easy to judge others. From contest shows to reality television, we are constantly encouraged to assess other people against ourselves. We are judged every day by how we look, how we talk, the jobs we have, and the schools we attend. We judge others by the same standards, often promoting or demoting ourselves based on an unrealistic cultural ideal.

This is especially true for believers in Christ. From God's Word, we learn a model for being in the world, yet not being of it. As a result, it becomes even more difficult for those who know the Lord to refrain from judging others and especially ourselves against this divine calling. If we are not careful, God's standard can be used as a weapon of death and punishment rather than an extension of life and grace.

Paul addressed this challenge of living up to a sacred standard without using it as a weapon against others in Romans. In the first chapter, he spelled out the consequences of sin, but he chased that in the second chapter with an admonition not to judge. Why? Because when we judge and condemn others, we also judge and condemn ourselves.

While condemnation is the way of the world, it is not the way of Christ. Jesus died to release us from condemnation and grant us entry to eternal life in him (Romans 8:1). We are saved by grace and called not to judge, but to bear witness to God's truth in humility and love.

The nations are crying out for people, like you and me, who will uphold a standard without condemnation. Let us walk boldly into this ministry, beginning with ourselves. By recognizing our constant need for God, we can displace judgment and replace it with love.

Lord, help me to release all from judgment, starting with myself. Give me your courage to walk humbly, your grace for my faults, and your love to see others as you see them.

THIRD TUESDAY

Clinging through Crisis

Read Psalm 39

"I am silent; I do not open my mouth, for it is you who have done it. Remove your stroke from me; I am worn down by the blows of your hand." (39:9–10)

"God is good, all the time, and all the time, God is good!" The call and response from my church rang out, as it did every Sunday, with exuberance and joy. But this time, I struggled to add my voice to the congregational chorus. For just a few minutes before, I learned that one of our members had just lost their child.

We rejoiced together when their prayer for pregnancy was answered. We cried together when the child entered the world. We believed together at the baby's baptism. And now, we grieved together as the future we envisioned for this child had been cut short.

How can we declare God's goodness in the midst of suffering from God's hand? It was God who gave this child and God who took the child away. As I wrestled with the age-old question of why bad things happen to good people, I also confessed my anger at God who allowed such heartache.

David was also familiar with this kind of heartache. In this psalm, he cried out to God for mercy, knowing that the suffering he experienced came only from God. Yet, in the midst of this pain, David did the only thing he knew to do: he clung more closely to God.

No matter how painful our suffering may be, God still invites us to come closer. Our instincts may lead us further away, but the wounds of Jesus remind us that he is intimately aware of every pain. There is no pain we experience that God cannot understand and heal.

This season, Jesus presents us with an opportunity to cling more dearly to his wounds by letting go of our pain. As we understand why Christ suffered, we will gradually proclaim that God is, indeed, good all the time, and all the time, God is good.

God, I need you to draw me closer, especially my places of pain. Restore my weary heart and bring peace to my soul. There is no one I need more than you.

FOURTH WEDNESDAY

Bold Crazy Faith

Read Numbers 13:17–27

"...Be bold, and bring some of the fruit of the land." Now it was the season of the first ripe grapes. (13:20b)

Let's be honest: you have to be just a little bit crazy to have faith in Jesus Christ. It's crazy to believe in a Savior we've never seen. It's looney to think that this unseen God can see all of us at every turn, all at the same time. But the most insane part is the fact that it takes courage to have this kind of crazy faith. You have to be intentional to have ridiculous faith in God.

Fortunately for us, there were millions of courageously crazy believers who preceded us, which is both comforting and scary. People like Moses had faith in God to do things that had never been done before. Take this passage in Numbers, for example. It's one thing to send spies into the land, but it's another thing to ask them to bring back evidence of its fruitfulness in broad daylight. Mind you, these were not berries that could be slipped into a pocket. No, the grapes in the land were so large that a single cluster had to be carried on a pole between two people!

What kind of God would lead Moses to take such risk? One who would risk everything to lead them into a better life. Moses and the spies demonstrated that our crazy faith is backed by an incredible God. This bold and audacious God called the people to do something crazy just to prove the truth of God's promise.

The call to follow Jesus is the call to have faith in a way that makes us seem boldly insane. But the One who invites us to risky faith is the one who risked it all just for us. So be bold for God. Don't be afraid to appear just a little crazy because soon the world will see that the grapes are better on the other side.

Most Incredible God, grant us holy boldness to follow you in this season. Teach us not to lean on our understanding, but to courageously trust you, even when things feel insane.

FOURTH THURSDAY

More Than Meets the Eye

Read 2 Corinthians 4:16—5:5

[B]ecause we look not at what can be seen but at what cannot be seen; for what can be seen is temporary, but what cannot be seen is eternal. (4:18)

I'll never forget the day the doctor told me that I needed glasses. For years, I had prided myself on being the only one in my immediate family with perfect sight. Yet, for a variety of reasons, I was forced into a new reality in which I would need assistance to see what I needed to see.

It was a significant moment that required serious adjustment. I had to change my routines and embrace a new normal. Years later, I admit that I'm not always good about remembering my glasses, but I do whatever it takes because I want to see.

Engaging on the journey with Christ can be like being prescribed new glasses. Crucifixion and resurrection can cause you to see life in a whole new way. Before Christ, life can look natural, material, and temporary. What you see is what you get. But when we engage with God through the Holy Spirit, life begins to look less natural and more spiritual, less material and more immaterial, less temporary and more eternal.

Our spiritual lenses enable us to see what the world cannot see and pursue an eternal goal that is beyond anything we've ever experienced. However, we're not always good about seeing through spiritual eyes. When challenges arise, it's easy to focus on what we see and forget the value of what is unseen. But through the suffering of Christ, God invites us to put on our glasses again and see what must be seen.

We must see Jesus crucified so that we can see our trials as temporary. We must see Christ buried so that we can see the truth about closed doors. And by God's grace, we must see the Savior resurrected so that we will see the promise that awaits us in eternal life.

Lord, help us to see what must be seen. Keep us from being blinded by the things that are temporary, and open our hearts to receive the eternal. We want to see you.

FOURTH FRIDAY

Remember the Stones

Read Joshua 4:14–24

"When your children ask their parents in time to come, 'What do these stones mean?' then you shall let your children know, 'Israel crossed over the Jordan here on dry ground.'" (4:21b–22)

You don't have to be a researcher to know that the American Church is in decline. Nearly every denomination is in the midst of descent, both in relevance and in numbers. Those same studies often point to younger generations as the root of the problem. But what if younger people leaving the church is not the problem, but a merely a symptom of a deeper problem? What if the deeper problem isn't the church of tomorrow, but the people who make up the church today?

In our scripture reading, God spelled out the importance of generational discipleship. Those who walked with God were to tell the stories of God's deliverance to others who did not know about it. This assumed that the younger generations would be curious enough to ask, but it also assumed that parents would speak regularly of the stones that reminded them of God's miraculous work.

No matter how old we are or how long we've walked with the Lord, all of us have stones and, as a result, all of us have stories. Stories are what keep values and traditions alive. Nearly every culture has stories that people pass on to maintain the narrative of who they are. From the way we cook to the meaning of the family name, every story has the power to shape the foundation for the next generation.

When was the last time you shared the story about your faith? It could be that the next generation is waiting to hear from you. In fact, the Lenten season can be a stone of its own. When people ask you why you read so diligently, or fast so faithfully, or pray so intentionally, perhaps the door will be opened for you to tell the story. By sharing, we lean into Christ as the Cornerstone and the ultimate symbol of God's faithfulness and love.

Holy Spirit, open our eyes to see the stones of your faithfulness, deliverance, and love. When you do, give us courage to tell the story so that coming generations may know the Lord.

FOURTH SATURDAY

A Reason to Rejoice

Read Psalm 32

Happy are those whose transgression is forgiven, whose sin is covered. (32:1)

What does it mean to be forgiven? Does it mean that my wrong can be turned into right? Could it mean that what I've done no longer counts against me? Surrounded by excuses and misappropriations of grace, we can miss an opportunity to rejoice if we don't take the time to understand what forgiveness really means.

The Hebrew term for "forgiveness" in this text means to lift, to bear up, to carry, or to take. The psalmist rejoiced because God lifted, bore, carried, and took the sin that weighed so heavily upon him. The term for "covered" is the same word used to describe the waters that covered the earth during the season of the flood in Genesis 7. King David, who composed this psalm, felt blessed because God had covered his sin as the waters had once covered the earth.

When we really think about the significance of divine forgiveness, we see that God has done more than just sweep our sin away. God lifted the weight that tried to bring us down; God bore the shame that we deserved; God carried the pain that we should own; God took the penalty that was meant for us. God covered our sin and became our hiding place. God protected us from the punishment we earned and had compassion when it seemed that no one else cared.

This is why we are called to rejoice. When we truly understand what it means to be forgiven, we can appreciate that God sent Jesus so that we, like David, can rejoice. Our happiness comes from knowing that God loves us enough to release us from the stigma of sin and free us from the prison of its shame. We are blessed when we recognize that Christ physically gave it all so that we might spiritually have it all.

It's time to let go of whatever keeps you from rejoicing today. No matter what else is happening, you have been forgiven, and that is a good reason to celebrate!

Jesus, thank you for forgiving us of our sins and cleansing us of all unrighteousness. Help us to always remember the significance of your mercy and grace.

FOURTH SUNDAY

The Not-So-Prodigal Child

Read Luke 15:1–3, 11b–32

"Then the father said to him, 'Son, you are always with me, and all that is mine is yours. But we had to celebrate and rejoice, because this brother of yours was dead and has come to life; he was lost and has been found.'" (15:31–32)

As an older child, I've always struggled with the parable of the prodigal son. I mean, why does the rebellious younger son get the party while the faithful one gets…well, nothing? Of course, we know that the older son had the father with him at all times, but that somehow doesn't seem to make it all right.

I was critical of the parable until I had a conversation with a mentor. He shared a pivotal moment in his leadership journey when he had to let a key person go. "When it was all over, I could feel the eyes of everyone else in the organization watching me. That's when it hit me: the way you let an employee go speaks volumes to the people who remain."

If we consider this principle in light of the parable, then perhaps the way the father welcomed the prodigal son spoke volumes to the faithful one who remained. What the father did for the younger son was not just for him. Maybe what the father did for the prodigal was to send a message of love and security to the older son as well.

Truthfully, none of us is the older child all the time. When we regularly place ourselves in the position of the older, faithful child, God gently reminds us that we will all identify with the prodigal child. At some point in our lives, we will make poor choices and fall short of God's grace. The only one who is the true and faithful Son at all times is Jesus Christ, and he never complained.

So let's celebrate the One who's been faithful since the beginning of time. Let's honor God who welcomes us home, no matter how long we've been away. And if you find yourself in a season of faithfulness, allow God's mercy to be a wink of affirmation that when you stray, God will do the same for you, too.

Lord, thank you for welcoming us when we stray and affirming us when we remain. Teach us to extend this mercy to each other in the same way you've extended it to us.

FOURTH MONDAY

Holy Sacrifice, Holy Rest

Read Leviticus 23:26–41

...and you shall do no work during that entire day; for it is a day of atonement, to make atonement on your behalf before the LORD your God. (23:28)

The Day of Atonement, known as Yom Kippur, is the holiest day of the year for the Jewish people. During the time of the temple, it was the only day when priests were allowed to enter the Holy of Holies to intercede on behalf of the people. On this day, the priests would slaughter an animal to atone or compensate for the sins of the people.

On this holy day, the people of Israel were instructed to deny themselves and to consecrate their bodies. They were to seek the Lord through prayer and fasting, rending their hearts in solemn repentance. Yet in the midst of all of this, they were called to do no work. On the Day of Atonement, they were to abide by the Sabbath, lest they be cut off from the community.

For this reason, the Day of Atonement is also known as the Sabbath of Sabbaths. It underscores the idea that the divine work of atonement does not need human activity. Otherwise stated, there is nothing you can do to help God compensate for your sins. Only God can atone for our sins; therefore, Christ can be the sacrifice.

Jesus atoned for our sins on the cross, once and for all. This means that there is nothing we can do to earn forgiveness or to work for grace. We are simply called to obedience through surrender and rest, as we consider the sacrifice of Christ. By resting, we honor the fact that nothing we can do would fix human brokenness.

What would it look like for you to rest in recognition of Christ's sacrifice? The call to honor God's atonement is also the call to Sabbath rest. In this time of holy consecration, let us cease from striving and rest in knowing that Jesus has paid it all.

God, we reverence the sacrifice of your Son as payment for our sin. Give us strength to rest, and keep us from trying to work for our own righteousness.

FOURTH TUESDAY

"Everybody Plays the Fool"

Read Psalm 53

Fools say in their hearts, "There is no God." They are corrupt, they commit abominable acts; there is no one who does good. (53:1)

> *"Everybody plays the fool sometime.
> There's no exception to the rule."*

These wise words rang out on the radio for the first time in 1972. The group was called the Main Ingredient, and although they were singing about falling in love, David sang it first about following God.

The godless are those who commit unfathomable acts. They are the ones who constantly do wrong, have no desire for right, and refuse to seek divine wisdom. But before our minds begin to list the people we know who fall into this category, the psalmist reminds us that everybody plays the fool when it comes to following God.

We become fools when we act as if there is no God and live as if God does not exist. Like the people of Israel, we may pledge our allegiance to the Lord in our hearts, but if our ways do not match up, the psalm reminds us that we are no different from the evil ones.

David found hope in the fact that God would bring deliverance one day. At the appointed time, he believed God would redeem God's people and restore their joy. With restoration would come wisdom, and those who acted as though they did not know God would be restored to eternal relationship with the Divine.

As God's New Testament people, we know that Christ is our deliverance, and through him we can experience a restored relationship with God. We may still occasionally play the fool, but we have realized hope in Jesus as our Savior. This hope gives us strength to seek wisdom and to live in a way that honors this sacred covenant.

Jesus, thank you for delivering us from our own foolishness. If we are fools, let us be fools for you. Make us bold witnesses of your power to restore.

FIFTH WEDNESDAY

Just Ask

Read 2 Kings 4:1–7

He said, "Go outside, borrow vessels from all your neighbors, empty vessels and not just a few." (4:3)

It's easy to miss out on God's blessing when we are not willing to ask for help. It may seem like a small thing, but admitting to a need can be a hurdle few are willing to jump. Our false assumptions about how we're supposed to live can prevent us from confessing when things are wrong.

We rationalize our seclusion, thinking that we are adults, and adults are supposed to take care of themselves. We are smart, and smart people should know better. Or worse yet, we are Christians, and Christians are supposed to give charity, not receive it.

In this beautiful story in 2 Kings, God connected the blessing to the woman's willingness to ask those around her for help. The only way to get empty vessels was to borrow them from the neighbors. This was a major risk. Doing so meant confessing that she did not have what she was supposed to have. But not asking could have cost her everything, including her children.

Girded by the words of the prophet and propelled by her desire to live, the woman did what many of us struggle to do: she asked for help from those around her. When she did, God provided for her in miraculous ways, giving her more than she ever imagined.

Sometimes, dependence on God will require some dependence on people. This kind of vulnerability can feel overwhelming, until we remember the vulnerability of Christ. Throughout his life, Jesus allowed himself to receive support from others, even when there was a chance they'd let him down.

If Christ lives in you, then you can be vulnerable too. Who's to say that there aren't empty vessels waiting in the storehouses of people you know? All you have to do is ask.

Lord, teach us that holy surrender includes occasions for human dependence. Give us boldness to ask and to believe that you will bring blessings for those who give and those who receive.

FIFTH THURSDAY

From the Self to The Savior

Read Philippians 2:19–24

I have no one like him who will be genuinely concerned for your welfare. All of them are seeking their own interests, not those of Jesus Christ. (2:20–21)

Sadly, there are very few people we can count on to genuinely care about others. Over the years, we've shaped a culture that rewards the narcissist while spurning the altruist. Those who think of themselves first can easily gain power, wealth, and social influence. Those who constantly put others first tend to get little recognition, earn lower pay, and may have marginal influence.

In today's environment, finding a person who authentically cares is like finding a rare jewel. When we are blessed to know them, we must treasure and protect them. These are our teachers who go above and beyond to nurture students. These are our custodians who take care of our facilities as if they were their own. These are our pastors and leaders who make sacrifices just to meet our needs.

This is how the apostle Paul felt about Timothy. Although he had many spiritual children and co-laborers in the ministry, Paul did not ascribe the same worth to them all. He may have had many who could preach and many others who could administer. But when it came to the gift of providing compassionate care, Timothy was the only one.

Why was Timothy so unlike the others? Paul suggested it was because he sought the interests of Christ and not of himself. When we truly get to know Christ, we understand that he was most interested in the will of God and the redemption of God's people. Stated simply, *we* are the interests of Jesus. Compassionate care for others comes from this rich understanding of the Savior's unconditional love for us.

Our world could use a few more people like Timothy. The only way we'll get there is by releasing our own interests in exchange for that which interests Christ: the salvation and redemption of the world.

Lord, we confess that our interests have not always been yours. Give us your heart for the world and teach us to care for others as you so deeply care for us.

FIFTH FRIDAY

From Midnight Sorrow to Morning Joy

Read Psalm 126

May those who sow in tears reap with shouts of joy. Those who go out weeping, bearing the seed for sowing, shall come home with shouts of joy, carrying their sheaves. (126:5–6)

Sometimes, midnight lingers longer than a night. In seasons of midnight turmoil, we can wonder if morning will ever come. Tears flow without ceasing. Mourning blankets the new day. Sorrow taints the windows of light. Grief clouds the vision of eyes yearning to see. Sometimes the darkness is so real that daylight seems like a distant reality.

Seasons of unexpected loss, trauma, and pain can provoke all sorts of despair. For the believer, despair is summed up in the inability to see beyond. We experience despair when we cannot see beyond the layoff, beyond the divorce, beyond the death, or beyond the suffering. When we cannot see beyond what is in front of us, we risk losing hope in the promise of redemption.

God's divine redemption is built on the premise that everything lost can be regained, sometimes in even greater measure. When God restores what was lost, we experience the resurgence of joy, the rekindling of love, and the resurrection of life, both natural and eternal. God's redemption is a reminder that "the Spirit of him who raised Jesus from the dead dwells in you" (Romans 8:11a).

If God is able to restore and redeem anything that we consider loss, then there is no such thing as empty suffering. With Christ, even our suffering is redeemed, giving us hope that there are new routes waiting at the end of every dead end. Perhaps this is why the psalmist sang that we can enter in sorrow and depart in joy. Through the lens of divine redemption, the tears we sow can, indeed, reap shouts of joy.

What would it look like for you to embrace your loss and lean into God's redemption? While everything within you tries to push away the pain, the Holy Spirit invites us to draw it in. Those who bring their tears into God's presence make room for the joy that is promised ahead.

Holy God, teach us to embrace our tears with hopeful expectation. May our moments of sorrow reap immeasurable joy, both now and in the seasons to come.

FIFTH SATURDAY
Redeeming Truth

Read John 11:45–57

But one of them, Caiaphas, who was high priest that year, said to them, "You know nothing at all! You do not understand that it is better for you to have one man die for the people than to have the whole nation destroyed." (11:49–50)

They were trying to calculate the risks. If they did nothing, Jesus would start a revolution and further incite the Romans against the Jewish people. If they got rid of Jesus, there was a chance the movement would be stopped and things would return to normal. In what he perceived was conventional wisdom, Caiaphas urged them to spare the nation by taking the life of one man. Ironically, this was exactly what God had in mind.

Throughout the scriptures, God demonstrates the ability to redeem evil motives and actions for good. God turned Joseph's enslavement into an opportunity for salvation. God turned Esther's captivity into a chance for communal vindication. And in the case of Jesus, God turned the vengeance of a small group into the redemption of the whole world.

Perhaps this explains why God does not always prevent the advance of sinful plans against us. The same God who did not stop the evil intentions of the enemy is the One who has power to turn everything around for good. Unbeknownst to those against us, their plans are still part of God's ultimate plan. Their worst intentions become part of the best intentions God had in mind all along.

When evil plans appear to advance in our lives and in the world, God calls us to remember the irony of the cross. What was designed to be a tool for death became the symbol of redemption and life. Knowing God's redemptive power through Christ should cause us to laugh at the troubles that try to take us down. Like a trampoline at the bottom of a pit, God uses whatever sends us spiraling downward to catapult us higher into God's victorious plan.

Instead of shying away from weapons formed against us, we rejoice with knowledge that they will not prosper. Let the words of those who seek our demise be turned into ironic phrases of triumph and truth.

In times of opposition, help us to see the truth of your redemption. Thank you for working things out for our good.

FIFTH SUNDAY

All Things New

Read Isaiah 43:16–21

I am about to do a new thing; now it springs forth, do you not perceive it? I will make a way in the wilderness and rivers in the desert. (43:19)

"What was" can pose as the enemy of "what can be." By nature, we have a tendency to hang onto the certainty of what was, rather than to lean into the ambiguity of what could be. This is especially true when the past wasn't all that bad.

If our method of doing things worked out before, we can sometimes struggle to conceive of a new way. This is where the old adage comes in: if it ain't broke, don't fix it. But sometimes, what lies at the source of this posture is fear. What has been is known, but what can be is unknown. The fear of the unknown brings many of its cousins, including fear of failure, fear of rejection, fear of loneliness, and even fear of success.

This is the soft spot that God touched in our text today. God introduced the promise of restoration and redemption with the guarantee of a brand-new way. If Israel thought the Red Sea was a big deal, they were in for a divine surprise. As Isaiah saw with his spiritual eyes, God was shaping a broader redemption for a larger group of people. God was preparing Jesus as the way in the wilderness and as the life-giving stream in the desert of the world.

Although the old ways were good, the new ways would have greater impact. What was done before laid the foundation for greater things to come. In this passage, God reminds us that what lies ahead with Christ is always better than what came before. All we have to do is be willing to perceive it.

See yourself leaning into the newness of Christ for your future by letting go of how God worked in the past. Though your eyes may not see it, let your heart be open to perceive the new things that God has prepared for you in Christ Jesus.

Open the eyes of our hearts, Lord. Help us to see you in the newness of life, and prepare us for the glorious things you have in store.

FIFTH MONDAY

The Anchor of Hope

Read Hebrews 10:19–25

Let us hold fast to the confession of our hope without wavering, for he who has promised is faithful. (10:23)

"I've been waiting for God for years and nothing has happened. I'm beginning to wonder if I've been a fool to trust a God who has yet to answer my prayers." I fought to hold back tears as I read my friend's Facebook post. He was a minister and desperately wanted to believe in God. While many would judge him and accuse him of spiritual weakness, I felt his pain and knew that God was not afraid of his doubts.

For better or worse, my friend's experience is not inconsistent with those who dared to trust God in scripture. Abraham believed God, and it was 400 years before the vision of the promised land came to light. Moses believed but never got to see the land for which he longed. Hebrews 11 gives us a laundry list of names of those who waited on God for years and never saw the visions fulfilled within their lifetimes.

What is the point of believing in God when the promises may not come to fruition? Perhaps the point is the journey itself. A perceived destination can distract us from seeing God's glory along the way. While the Jews were focused on the Messiah as a destination, Jesus came alongside as the Messiah of the journey. Christ's aim was not simply the redemption of one group of people on earth, but the salvation of anyone who believed—from all nations, for all generations.

The journey with Jesus is itself a destination. The presence of God with us gives us hope in God's promise. Though the outcomes may be uncertain, Christ lives with us to prove that God is consistently faithful in companionship. Holding fast to our hope doesn't mean we won't have doubts. It just means that we trust the "who" of the promise, even when we cannot see the "what."

God, restore our hope in you as the Faithful Promise Giver. Remind us that your Word is true, even when it takes time to emerge.

FIFTH TUESDAY

Reposition Your Pride

Read Psalm 20

Some take pride in chariots, and some in horses, but our pride is in the name of the LORD our God. (20:7)

"In God We Trust" is the most recognizable phrase printed on American currency. It is the official motto of our nation and is inscribed on the face of our greatest temptation: money. While we no longer have chariots and few depend on horses, all of us need money to survive.

The tension between God and money is nothing new. Even Jesus recognized this tension in the disciples, reminding them that no one can serve two masters (Matthew 6:24). While money is designed to be a tool for our use, we can twist things around by becoming tools for money to use. Rather than making our money work for us, we can find ourselves working for the money. This is true even within the church.

As we continue to reach for more in life, we can unintentionally allow wealth to be the singular indicator of our success. But David's prayer for victory was measured differently from the success of the world. This countercultural call invites us to take pride and find strength in God alone. Other nations may boast in what they have, but we are called to boast in who we know.

On the cross, Christ radically upended our perception of strength. Becoming weak in his death, Jesus made it possible for us to become strong. In his triumph over the grave, Christ made us rich with new life. This is why we take pride in the name of the Lord who saved, redeemed, and renamed us by his blood.

Perhaps it's time to take an honest assessment of the chariots and horses in our lives. Have we mistakenly put our trust in what we possess instead of trusting in the One who possesses us? In this season, we are called to re-anchor ourselves in Christ as the unparalleled source and strength of our lives.

We confess that we have misplaced our trust and taken pride in things that don't ultimately matter. Lord of Heaven, resume your place as Master and Source of our lives. You are our strength and our pride.

SIXTH WEDNESDAY

Hindsight Grace

Read Luke 18:31–34

But they understood nothing about all these things; in fact, what he said was hidden from them, and they did not grasp what was said. (18:34)

The disciples didn't get it, but who can fault them? Jesus told them everything about his death and resurrection, but they were kept from understanding it. His words may have been plainly spoken, but they were beyond human comprehension. They had ears but did not hear, just as the Messiah anticipated.

So if Jesus knew they would not understand, why did he take the time to explain it to them? Maybe he wasn't explaining things to them at all. Perhaps Luke recorded an experience in retrospect in order for Christ to explain it to us. Although they didn't get it then, a retrospective look can reveal the intentionality of God's plan.

Looking back on the events leading up to the cross, Luke remembered that Jesus knew exactly what would happen. He did his best to prepare the disciples, even if it meant they wouldn't understand it at the time. Being in full control of his life, he willingly went to the cross. Though the process would be traumatic for Jesus and for the disciples, these words let them know that the course was anticipated and that Jesus was prepared.

Occasionally, we are invited to look back at the traumatic moments of our lives and see how God prepared us, even when we did not understand. The gift of hindsight allows us to see from the past what we could not perceive in the present. When we take a backward look, we will likely see God's grace working in ways we did not understand at that time.

There are authentic moments when we cannot process what happens at the time it occurs. Some events are so traumatic that the significance is hidden from us, as it was for the disciples. By leaning into God's grace in the moment, we can let go of our need to understand fully. After all, some things are only clear after the fact.

Jesus, thank you for hindsight grace. Teach us to let go of our need to know now. Prepare us for the day when we will know and be known in your presence forever.

SIXTH THURSDAY

Exchanging the Law for Life

Read Hebrews 2:1–9

For if the message declared through angels was valid, and every transgression or disobedience received a just penalty, how can we escape if we neglect so great a salvation? (2:2–3a)

There is no way to rationalize the divine trade. No matter how you slice it, his life for ours will never come out even. The predominance of sin in our lives and in the world makes it impossible for us to live perfectly, even with the power of the Holy Spirit working within.

Our good deeds vanish in the shadow of our wrongs. Our moments of sincerely turning to God are matched by the moments when we intently turn away. We will never be good enough, strong enough, capable enough, or worthy enough to merit Christ's giving his life for us.

But he decided to do it anyway. With the scales drastically imbalanced and the odds stacked against us, Christ still tasted death for our sins so that we wouldn't have to. It makes no sense to pay billions for something worth no more than a dime, and yet the Savior still died for sinners like you and me. How do we reconcile this unjust exchange?

The writer of Hebrews suggests that we reconcile the weight of this message with full acceptance and belief in the truth of the Gospel. If the law affirmed by the Old Testament is true, then salvation through Jesus in the New Testament is even more true.

When we begin to understand the significance of the law, we will see the powerful implications of the cross. This revelation alone has power to change the way we live: not as perfect people, but as those who have been redeemed. Not as entitled generations, but as grateful ones saved by grace through faith.

We can respond to the significance of the cross by letting go of what we think we deserve and embracing what we truly deserved: death for our sins. By plunging into the validity of the law, we can emerge with legitimate joy in the Good News.

"What Thou, my Lord, hast suffered was all for sinners' gain; mine, mine was the transgression, but Thine the deadly pain. Lo, here I fall, my Savior! 'Tis I deserve Thy place; look on me with Thy favor, vouchsafe to me Thy grace." (from the hymn "O Sacred Head Now Wounded")

SIXTH FRIDAY

Don't Wait for the Rainbows

Read Isaiah 54:9–10

This is like the days of Noah to me: Just as I swore that the waters of Noah would never again go over the earth, so I have sworn that I will not be angry with you and will not rebuke you. (54:9)

The story of Noah and the ark is anything but a children's book. The people living during that time stirred God's wrath so much that God opted to completely destroy them with a flood. Our plush toys and children's church programs sadly miss the mark by glorifying the tragedy of God's endeavor to start again.

Triggered by human wickedness and provoked by the extent of evil on earth, God regretted the creation of humankind. This was a painful realization, one that grieved God's heart. But the moment of redemption came when Noah found favor in God's eyes.

In our reading today, Isaiah invites us to linger a little longer on the story of Noah. While the context may have changed, the capacity of the human heart remains the same. The propensity to do evil and wickedness is very much alive in our world. What prevents God from wiping us out as he did before? A covenant of love solidified by Jesus, God's Son.

In Genesis, the sign of the covenant appeared as a rainbow. It became a visible reminder that God would never destroy us by flood again. Isaiah prophesied a covenant of peace as a symbol of God's unrelenting love. And in the New Testament, Jesus became the embodied covenant of God, the reminder of God's commitment to love and preserve us by grace.

Life's struggles can sometimes cloud our view of God's covenant of love. Hardship and pain can veil God's compassion, making it hard to see the sunlight through the clouds. But, while we cannot always see the rainbows, we can always see the cross. By letting go of momentary symbols, we can lean more deeply into the covenant of Christ, a covenant that solidifies the steadfastness of God's love, no matter what life may bring.

God, thank you for preserving our lives through Christ. Give us the ability to lean into your covenant and to walk with the assurance of your presence.

SIXTH SATURDAY

In God's Hands

Read Psalm 31:9–16

My times are in your hand; deliver me from the hand of my enemies and persecutors. (31:15)

In the 1950s, an AllState Insurance Company executive came up with the popular slogan "You're in good hands with AllState." He told the company that he came up with this idea after trying to assure his wife that their child was in good hands with the doctor. What started as a moment of comfort for a family turned into a mantra of security for a company that is still widely recognized today.

David also understood the benefits of being "in good hands." Long before car insurance came along, the psalmist reiterated the importance of facing difficulties with proper protection. When his enemies and persecutors tried to seize his life in their hands, the king reminded himself that he was firmly within God's grasp. He did not have to fear the grip of his enemies because his life, seasons, and times were wrapped in the safety of God's control.

It takes courage to entrust yourself into God's hands. After all, these were the very hands that allowed the Messiah to be crucified. How can we entrust ourselves to God when a positive outcome is not always guaranteed? Perhaps we can trust God's hands when we understand God's heart.

The cross provides a powerful look at the depth of God's heart for the world. By sending Jesus to die for us, we understand God's relentless love that will do anything just to save us. Knowing that God will do anything to save us provides assurance against the attacks of the enemy. In God's hands, we have the full protection of the One who shed blood to secure our freedom.

Stop trying to take matters into your own hands and lean more fully into God's capable hands. By resting in God, we can learn to hear the heartbeat of love that protects us from the ultimate enemy of eternal death.

Holy Spirit, give us grace to lean into your capability and let go of our control. Hold us tightly in your grip. Thank you for the assurance that you will not let us go.

LITURGY OF THE PALMS SUNDAY

The Laws of Divine Physics

Read Luke 19:28–40

He answered, "I tell you, if these were silent, the stones would shout out." (19:40)

Newton's Third Law tells us, "For every action, there is an equal and opposite reaction." This law is based on the idea that there are equal and opposite forces working together in every interaction. Though subtle, this law is prevalent and can be observed in all of nature and even in our own lives through cause and effect.

What is interesting about today's reading is the subtle implication of the laws of physics. In responding to the Pharisees who asked him to silence the praise of his disciples, Jesus introduced a law of his own. If the disciples did not offer praise, nature would be compelled to act. The action of Christ's triumphal entry required an equal and opposite reaction of praise.

We cannot underestimate what it meant that Jesus entered Jerusalem in triumph. Throughout his years, the Savior lived a near clandestine life. He wove his way through the scenes, trying not to disrupt the cosmos too much before his time. He silenced those who wanted to talk about him and hardly ever made public displays of his lordship. But on this occasion, he held nothing back.

The heavens could hold it no longer. The earth had grown weary of keeping it in. Sooner or later, someone or something had to react to God Incarnate. Silence was not an option during this celebration because the lordship of Jesus merited loud and boisterous praise. The cause of Christ provoked an effect worthy of a king.

According to these laws, our mere existence warrants praise. The breath we breathe must be returned to God in thanksgiving. The act of leaning into God's presence results in a natural reaction of peace and joy. Our very lives call for shouts of joy that must come from somewhere, even if it happens to be a stone.

God, we acknowledge that your presence requires praise. We praise you for triumphant victory through Christ. Let our lives reflect just a portion of the glory you deserve.

HOLY WEEK MONDAY

The Narrow View of Justice

Read Isaiah 42:1–9

He will not cry or lift up his voice, or make it heard in the street; a bruised reed he will not break, and a dimly burning wick he will not quench; he will faithfully bring forth justice. (42:2–3)

The journey to the cross can feel like a shrinking entryway. The ceiling gets lower with every step as the walls come in and the path narrows. The closer we get, the lower we must stoop until we find ourselves crawling on our hands and knees, face to the ground, in an attempt to catch a glimpse of the Suffering Servant.

The exuberant joy of Palm Sunday feels like a distant memory. All we can see now is the face of Jesus set firmly toward Calvary. The tensions of the Savior are now fully in play. Christ is both weak and strong, vulnerable and capable, fully human and fully divine.

This dichotomy stands out not only for what Jesus will endure, but also for the type of people he has come to save. His weakness builds solidarity with the weak; his silence coincides with those who have no voice. Though he has all power, he does not abuse it. Though he has all knowledge, he does not vilify the ignorant. Christ is on a mission, and if we look closely enough for long enough, we will see that the mission of the cross is justice.

The cross initiates faithful justice where the last become first and the marginal become central. Unlike earthly justice, Christ's work will bring lasting equity for sinners in need of grace. This is good news for every nation. Christ has come to level the scales of life and death, good and evil, once and for all.

The pathway is narrowing and we will not clearly see the fullness of the justice mission on earth. But the promise of Christ through the cross is a promise of wider vision on the other side. On the way there, we'll need to let go of the extra baggage and shed any unnecessary weight. As we do, we just might find ourselves leaning in for a view we've never experienced before.

Christ Jesus, help us to lean in. Give us strength to let go of anything that keeps us from a closer view. We want to see justice play out through your eyes.

HOLY WEEK TUESDAY

Resisting the Rational

Read 1 Corinthians 1:18–31

For the message about the cross is foolishness to those who are perishing, but to us who are being saved it is the power of God. (1:18)

Paul was considered the best in his class. He had all of the attributes of a successful Pharisee. In devout faithfulness, he kept the tenets of the law. He even referred to himself as a "Hebrew of Hebrews," consistent in his practices and integrous in his application.

This was the kind of life upheld by those in his community. His values merited success. His dedication warranted praise. His wisdom called for honor and recognition. But when Paul encountered Jesus, none of that carried any weight. It mattered only as much as it was surrendered to Christ through the cross.

When Jesus came to earth, he ushered in a season of disruption; its effect rippled across every nation, throughout the ages. The Savior's coming disrupted every system, shaking the foundation of religious tradition in every way. Those who were esteemed in the faith were abased by the cross. Those who were lifted high in the law were brought low before the cross. Jesus literally turned life upside down and presented a view of God that was anything but what the pious had imagined.

Because of the cross, we now walk in the truth, a truth that is counter to nearly everything on earth. Through Christ, we find our lives by losing them, we gain treasure by giving it away, and we rise only as much as we are willing to fall. This is absolute madness for unbelieving ears. It's irrational and silly to believe that one man's death would be an exchange for so many.

But this message of foolishness is the message by which we live. It is the message of the Gospel that saves and redeems us, just as it did for Paul. So it's time to let go of our rational ideas of faith. Leaning into the insensibility of the cross is the only way we'll make sense of God's work in our lives.

Heavenly God, we confess our tendency to accept only what seems reasonable. Disarm us with your wisdom and make us fools for Christ.

HOLY WEEK WEDNESDAY

Betrayed and Redeemed

Read John 13:21–32

After saying this Jesus was troubled in spirit, and declared, "Very truly, I tell you, one of you will betray me." (13:21)

It's a painful experience to be betrayed. The process of building trust takes so long that betrayal seems to cut to the core. This is especially true for those close to us. Although we can stand being forsaken by those on the fringe, it is agonizing when a friend turns on us.

True friendships are often fortified in the furnace of opposition, and the disciples had plenty of that. They survived being criticized for leaving their careers to follow the "untrained" Rabbi. They endured the shock of witnessing countless miracles they never could have imagined. They even persevered through name-calling, being ostracized by the religious leaders, and being considered frauds by everyone else.

Their experiences bonded them together like glue. With all they had left behind, they were more than just friends, they were like family. But during one of the most intimate family gatherings, Jesus announced to his brothers that one of them would betray him.

Who would dare disrupt this family bond? A better question might be, who wouldn't? We know that Judas betrayed Christ in the most obvious way, but every single one of the disciples betrayed him as well. In the heat of the torture, this ragtag family fell apart, each one deserting the Savior in some way.

It is wise for us to consider the many ways we, too, have betrayed our Lord. We may not all be as blatant as Judas, but we have all troubled Christ by our desertion. Yet the cross provides a powerful antidote for those who betray. Forgiveness and mercy are ours through the shed blood of Jesus, making us family once again.

Let us honor Christ's sacrifice by naming our betrayal and laying our shame down at the foot of the cross. Then we can emerge as a family, not of betrayers, but of those who are redeemed.

Jesus, we, whom you have called family, have betrayed you in far too many ways. In your mercy, give us grace to repent and turn back to you once again. Thank you for redeeming our souls.

MAUNDY THURSDAY

Engage Your Senses

Read Exodus 12:1–14

The blood shall be a sign for you on the houses where you live: when I see the blood, I will pass over you, and no plague shall destroy you when I strike the land of Egypt. (12:13)

I once had the privilege of traveling to modern-day Samaria. Located in the West Bank, the people in this area consider themselves the "purest of the Jews" and can trace their lineage all the way back to Adam.

I was most intrigued by their consistent and elaborate practice of Passover. Each year, the families of Samaria gather at Mount Gerizim to slaughter lambs and worship God together. They don white clothing, chant traditional Jewish songs, and eat so there are no leftovers, as the Bible commands. As a smaller sect of Israel, they consider this ceremony a reminder that God will always protect a remnant and preserve their lineage.

The Exodus passages are read loudly for all to hear as people from all over the world put their hands together in prayer. The smell of the slaughter covers everything as the taste of a communal meal takes center stage.

The visible contrast of white clothes and red blood served, for me, as a sensory reminder of what Christ alone has done for us. Jesus became the sacrificial Lamb, and there would be no need for another. His blood was the sign of protection, and his body was given so that we may be spared. But in the transition from the Law to the Cross, the multisensory experience can get lost. We tend to only understand Christ on Maundy Thursday by what we see with our eyes and what we do with our hands.

Yet the call of Christ for those who yearn to draw near is to see, hear, taste, smell, and touch. Like Samaritans, we must lean in to experience the sacrifice with our eyes, ears, mouths, noses, and hands. This is an invitation to let go of an overdependence on sight and engage God with our whole being.

Holy Lamb of God, we long to know you in every way. Activate our senses so that we may connect our hearts more deeply to yours.

GOOD FRIDAY

Surveying the Wondrous Cross

Read Psalm 22

My God, my God, why have you forsaken me? Why are you so far from helping me, from the words of my groaning?... Yet you are holy, enthroned on the praises of Israel. (22:1,3)

It would have been easy to believe that Jesus was forsaken. According to the Gospel of Mark, Jesus had been suffering and suffocating on the cross for about six hours. This did not include the agony of his trial, the pain of the whips, or the distance he had to carry the wood for his cross.

Being nailed to that cross required long nails to be hammered through flesh, ligaments, and bone. Archeologists suggest that crucifixion required coarse ropes to be tied tightly around the arms, causing blood vessels to break, muscles to strain, and the head to droop down over the neck, gradually cutting off the air supply. The weight of his body would gradually drag down against the long, rusty nails, dragging his skin up and down the piercing splinters of wood.

The process of lifting himself to breathe would pull against the raw, torn holes in his hands and feet. Every breath required work that his weakened body could not handle. Yet even in this weakened state, the Savior found enough words to minister to each of us.

Declaring these words of agony proved that it is possible to be fully connected with God and feel fully forsaken at the same time. Harking back to Psalm 22, Jesus uttered the words of David and gave us strength to utter them as well.

While his breath could not speak more than one verse, there is no doubt that his mind remembered every single word. The one who felt forsaken was also the one who trusted God. As David matched his grief with hope, Jesus did the same by matching his despair with trust in God's holiness.

It is a powerful thing to name your despair and meet it with hope in Christ. As we lean into Christ's suffering, we let go of our own and recognize the true weight of his sacrifice.

Thank you, Jesus, for giving us permission to speak our pain. Let our breath end with a note of hope, believing that your life brings more life for us ahead.

HOLY SATURDAY

Everything Comes to Light

Read John 19:38–42

After these things, Joseph of Arimathea, who was a disciple of Jesus, though a secret one because of his fear of the Jews, asked Pilate to let him take away the body of Jesus…Nicodemus, who had at first come to Jesus by night, also came… (19:38a, 39a)

Saturday would have been a good day to hide. The drama of Christ's crucifixion was over, but fear still hung in the air. The lifeless body was proof of death, but the prophecy of resurrection was still whispered in the background. While the threat of a messianic takeover seemed nullified, the disruption he caused was real. There were blind people who could see, dead people who were alive, sick people who were healed, and many more miracles too numerous to count.

In the silence of Saturday, there was still noise. This noise against those who followed Jesus made the day after death a good day to disappear. Yet with all that was against them, two men refused to remain in the dark: Joseph of Arimathea and Nicodemus. Both considered themselves followers, even though they had previously hidden for fear of their lives. Yet both felt compelled to come out of hiding on the one day they had good reason to fear: the day after the Savior was crucified.

What drove them to come out after being hidden for so long? Was the request for his body so benign that they were confident no one would suspect their devotion? Perhaps they came forward because they had no other choice. Discipleship is costly and, thus far, it had not cost them very much. But when Christ gave his all, even secret disciples felt the need to come into the light. The boldness of the cross inspired a necessary boldness in them to care for the Savior.

Following Jesus will always cost us something. In our silent Saturdays, when it would be easier to hide in darkness, the cross reminds us that all things must come to light. The more we lean in, the more devoted we become. The more devoted we are, the more willingly we let go and risk our lives for the One who risked all for us.

God of Mercy, forgive us for hiding and for claiming Christ only when it is convenient. Thank you for your compassionate redemption. Make us true disciples.

EASTER VIGIL, EASTER SUNDAY

A New Song for a New Season

Read Psalm 98

O sing to the LORD a new song, for he has done marvelous things. His right hand and his holy arm have gotten him victory. (98:1)

Jesus defied the grave! He conquered death with life and opened the door to life everlasting. He proved to all that his words were true, and vindicated those who believed his Lordship. The stone was rolled away, and angels bore witness to the miraculous resurrection.

Jesus defied the grave! Instead of ending, our lives are now beginning. What should have been the final verse is now surpassed by a brand-new chorus. The cross was thought by many to be the last note, but our song continues with resurgent praise.

Jesus defied the grave! This is our new song to sing. The cross was meant for torture, and the grave once signified termination, but Jesus resisted them all. We will no longer sing songs that end in sorrow, because Christ has sealed our joy. God has always performed miracles, but through Jesus, God did the most marvelous thing: God redeemed our lives through the destruction of death.

Whatever seems dead can be resurrected with Christ. The doors that seem closed are no challenge for the Savior. The low points of life can be redeemed by the Blood, and nothing can separate us from God's unconditional love. For the right hand is God's power, and the holy arm, God's divine strength. Now our victory is secured by the power of God and the strength of our Almighty King.

Jesus defied the grave! What more do we have to fear? The ultimate price was paid to demolish death as the final frontier. If we choose not to sing, we choose not to believe, and risk minimizing the wonder of God.

Come, let us sing this new song! Let us lean in and let go. Armed with the triumph of the cross, we release every failure and cast down every ounce of defeat. Hallelujah, Christ is risen indeed!

Lord, we give you praise and glory for the miracle of resurrection! Your life gives us eternal life, and we can never thank you enough. May our lives ring forth with this new song so that others may hear and draw near to you.

RESURRECTION OF THE LORD

Will You Lean In?

Read John 20:1–18

He bent down to look in and saw the linen wrappings lying there, but he did not go in. (20:5)

Not everyone who approaches the empty tomb will go in. Some will get close enough to see, but not be willing to touch. Others will wait in fear, unsure of what will happen if they take another step. Still others will witness the miracle and refuse to get a closer look.

This is what happened on the day Christ was resurrected. There were two disciples running to the grave, but only one went in. Although John reached the site first, it was Peter who entered first while John stood on the outside. We can only speculate the reason for John's hesitation, but we know that something kept him from leaning in.

There's a chance that some have taken this Lenten journey and have yet to lean in. Perhaps, like John, there is something keeping us from getting a closer look. There may be vestiges of baggage we've yet to let go: fear that keeps us bound, pain still unresolved, wounds yet to be healed, or doubts that persist in our minds. We may not know what it is, but if we are standing by the empty tomb, we still have hope.

John may have resisted at first, but he remained long enough to make a new choice. After seeing Peter enter, he finally decided it was time to go in. At a certain point, John made the decision that leaning in was more important than holding on.

There is nothing more important than experiencing Jesus. Nothing we hold compares to what we can have in Christ. When we lean in to witness the resurrection, we experience the power that now lives within us. If we wait outside, we could miss our hope and deny what God has invested in us.

So take the leap. Make the choice. Lean into the reality of the risen Savior and experience the gift of immeasurable grace.

Precious Lord, take my hand. Lead me into the evidence of resurrection and help me to believe. May my path forward be better than anything I am leaving behind. In the name of Jesus, AMEN!

Color and connect
with the Bible in a fresh new way!

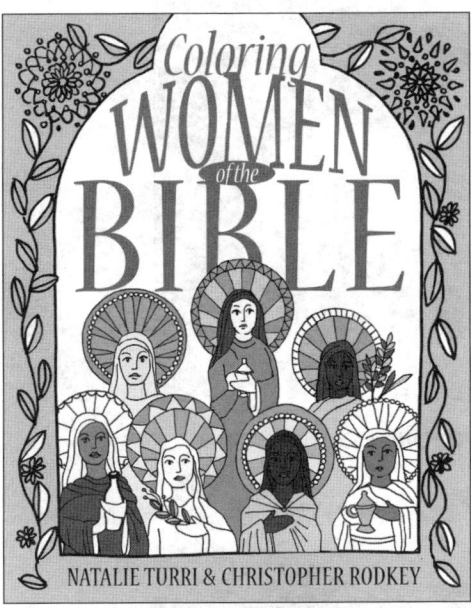

ISBN 9780827203983

FREE reflection guide includes plans for small groups, women's retreats, and personal use.

In these beautiful coloring book devotionals, experience the beloved stories and characters of the Bible anew. Great for personal use, intergenerational coloring, or coloring fellowship groups! Special prices for 5-and 10-book kits.

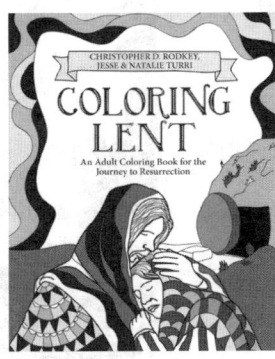

ISBN 9780827205475

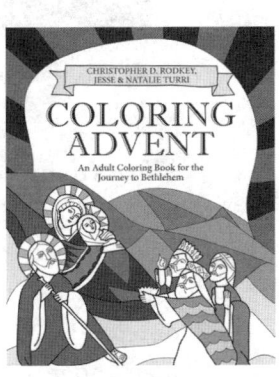

ISBN 9780827203976

ChalicePress.com/ColoringWomen   800-366-3383

Annual stewardship campaigns are about more than fundraising.

ISBN 9780827205444

Stewardship season is an opportunity to embrace the ministry your church does together. *Community of Prayer,* a daily devotional covering four weeks, helps your congregation think differently about stewardship and the power of their generosity.

Save 20% everyday when you buy at Chalice Press! Discounts on bulk orders.

ChalicePress.com   800-366-3383

Jesus was a lousy messiah.

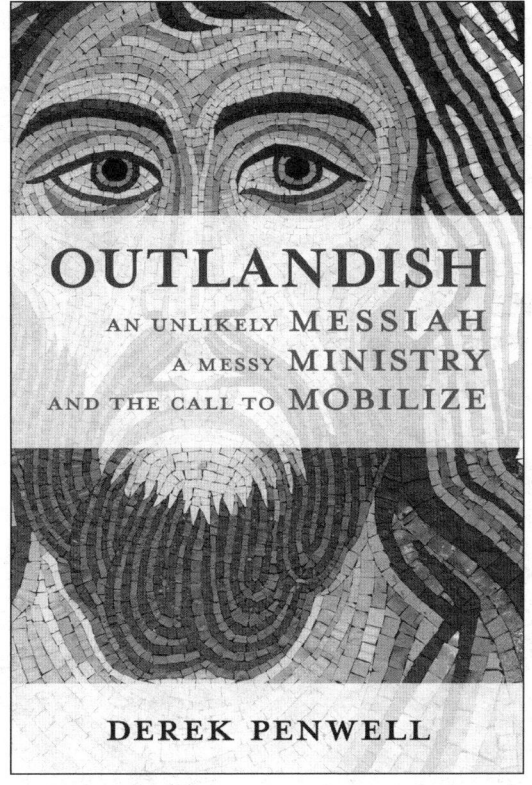

ISBN 9780827231665

Ministering to the wrong people. Angering the wrong people. Having outrageous expectations of his followers. Questionable teaching methods. A humiliating end followed by an improbable surprise ending. And then, somehow, inspiring millions to attempt to change the world in his name.

Outlandish shares the political, social, and organizational lessons of Jesus' radically different ministry and provides the tools for following him out into the world today.

Save 20% everyday when you buy at Chalice Press!

ChalicePress.com/Outlandish   800-366-3383

Women were made to lead. Everywhere.

ISBN 9780827223677

Made to Lead empowers you to live out your calling boldly and confidently. Draw closer to God with relevant biblical examples and heartfelt prayers. Break down stereotypes of women in leadership. And create your own successful reality in which you are a key part of God's holy community.

"Reading this book will not only help women in ministry to be unleashed but will unleash men to be partners in ministry and not competitors." —Rodney L. Cooper, Gordon-Conwell Theological Seminary

Save 20% everyday when you buy at Chalice Press!

ChalicePress.com   800-366-3383